The Culture and Perception Link, A Part of Us

Table of Contents

Introduction

This review of research literature discusses the salience of emotional aspects in relationships and environmental stimuli that could enhance and perpetuate the holistic perceptual tendency in collectivistic individuals. In an interdependent culture, relational harmony is valued and potential conflict between members is avoided. Sensitivity towards emotional cues and expressions of others could be beneficially fostered under the East Asian culture. Emotional dependence is also an observed tendency of those who are field-dependent. This suggests that the salience of emotional characteristics and cues in holistic perception affects field-dependent and East Asian individuals to a greater degree than analytical Westerners of an independent culture. Though the mechanism(s) is still unclear, it could be attributed to psychosocial factors. Moreover, a study that compared American and Japanese city scenes suggest the influence of a considerable amount of informational stimuli from background structures on visual perception. East Asians have also been found to exhibit broader attentional breadth and greater frequency of gaze saccades crossing between the object and background of pictures in visual experiments than Westerners. In order for future research to achieve a clearer understanding of the social basis of holistic perception in East Asians, the themes of increased sensitivity to implicit emotional states of others and constant visual exposure to one's external environment are worth considering. It can be said that perception is not a discrete function of the senses but a part of a complex web of information interchange involving the profound influence of psychosocial and external environmental realms of life.

Acknowledgement

The author would like to acknowledge that a major portion of this book content has been previously published in the University of British Columbia Undergraduate Journal of Psychology under the article title "The Influence of Emotion Saliency and Environmental Stimuli on Field Dependence and Holistic Perceptual Style."

Cultural psychology has contributed to our understanding of how psychological aspects of our culture vary according to their origins and practices around the world. Ancient civilizations developed their region-specific cultures which penetrated and influenced the daily lives of their people through communication and daily lifestyle practices. Our ability to perceive with our senses shares complex functional interconnections with other active mental capacities, in particular, cognition, attention and memory. The combined outcome of this rich network of internal information exchange circuit in perceiving and making sense of external stimuli serves to place humans, who are capable of high-fidelity cultural learning—that is, learning that involves efficient imitation of others based on well-developed language and theory-of-mind abilities, which are an advantage over other animals (Heine, 2010). Our attachment to the culture which influences us is a defining aspect of our identity.

Eastern and Western Cultural Roots

The interesting contrast between Western individualism and Eastern collectivism has attracted much research over the past few decades. In tracing back to their respective ancient Greek and Chinese philosophical roots, efforts have been made to explain the origin of such cultural divergence. Culture not only provides us with a structural framework for our content and conduct in communicating information, but it is also a lens through which certain aspects of our perception of interpersonal interaction are magnified or made less salient, such as by concentrating or diverting our focus of attention with long-time practice and adherence to acceptable norms. Our distinct cultural backdrop underlies the East-West dichotomy in the process of information perception and exchange, perpetuating their influence through familial interactions and along social and visual dimensions within our cultural environment.

Early studies on perceptual processing have led to the categorization of "field-independent" and "field-dependent" tendencies according to the extent to which one decontextualizes an object from its field (Witkin, Dyk, Faterson, Goodenough, & Karp, 1974). To explain differences in visual tendencies of certain occupational groups, Witkin and Berry (1975) proposed that those whose livelihood requires effective cooperative efforts and harmonious relations amongst fellow workers (e.g., farmers) are more field-dependent than those who are self-reliant and socially independent on the job (e.g., herders). This parallels the contrast between Eastern interdependent and Western independent societies (Norenzayan, Choi, & Peng, 2007). In ancient China, geographical features of the land allowed for extensive farming practice as compared with land-limited Greece, where the more autonomous and individualistic trade and fishing were common. Thus, the strong influence of Greek traditions and philosophy on the Western world suggests a basis for cultural promotion of field independence. Compared to Easterners, Westerners are able to separate visual target objects from their background with greater ease. This is described as analytic perceptual tendency that facilitates the perception of each object as an individual and discrete unit by categorisation according to object properties and abstract rules (Heine, 2012).

When East Asian participants underwent the Rod and Frame Test, in which they were presented with images of a rod against a distracting graphic background and then tested whether they were able to tell accurately the rod was tilted or vertically straight, they attended more to the entirety of visual information in the pictures shown to them. This led to difficulty and inaccuracy in detecting the rod's subtle angle of deviation from the horizontal and vertical. Such demonstration of a holistic perceptual style is distinguished from an analytic perceptual style. The extent to which they were basing their perception of the rod's position on the misleading graphic background demonstrated that they were more visually field-dependent. A study by Chua, Boland, and Nisbett (2005) reported that Chinese participants looked more at a distracting background instead of objects, similar to the case of the Rod and Frame Test. Therefore, it is the aim of this paper to further discuss two aspects of holistic perceptual style: (1) a relationship-oriented perception of collective objects of stimuli, which is exhibited by field dependence; and (2) an expanded scope of visual focus that takes into account not only the foreground but also the background of the field.

East Asians' Perception of Emotional Content

A study by Chua, Leu, and Nisbett (2005) found that adult Taiwanese participants described more emotional content than American participants in their recall of personal events and video clips that had been shown before engaging in distracter tasks. In another study (Masuda & Nisbett, 2001), Japanese participants were found to be more likely to perceive emotions in fish, when shown videos of them, than Americans. The salience of emotion to the Japanese participants in their perception of the objects' characteristics could be suggestive of a link between the emotional quality and interconnections among components within one's visual field. Since emotional perception plays a significant part in both verbal and implicit human social interactions, leading to purposeful and meaningful relationships, emotion as a property of visual objects may further enhance perception of their interaction with one another—an implication of a relationship that is active and ongoing.

Although the suppression of explicit emotional expression may be emphasized in East Asian cultures that value harmonious relations, reliance on emotional cues through alternative channel(s) to prevent potential conflict could be a motivation for developing acuity in perceiving implicit social messages attempted to be conveyed under restrained contexts. Kitayama and Ishii (2002) reported that Japanese participants, in comparison with American participants, exhibited more interference effect on their judgement accuracy of words spoken in a contradicting emotional tone. It can be observed that emotional voice tone may serve dissimilar verbal functions in the Western and Eastern worlds. It could be that Eastern traditional customs and etiquette associated with emotional vocal tone moderation are less explicitly defined than the suppression of emotional facial cues. On the one hand, it may be an adaptive strategy by members of a culture rooted in Confucianism, which encourages speech moderation, to communicate implicit information through variation in emotional vocal tone without compromising explicit verbal content.

While it is debatable whether such results exhibited by Japanese participants can be generalized to other East Asian cultural groups, it suggests the saliency of emotional significance in not only visual perception of characteristics of stimuli but also within the framework of social interaction that can serve as an adaptive function in conflict prevention and resolution. This shows that the underlying emotional quality of both speech and visual stimuli is more salient to holistic perceivers. Just as we have the tendency to detect a person's emotion by our perception of one's facial expression, the relationship between emotion and visual attention in terms of how malleable it is to psychosocial factors should be further explored. It is still unclear as to whether prioritization of emotional aspects by a culture leads to holistic perception or merely serves as an adjunct enhancer of such perceptual processing.

Field Dependence and Emotional Dependence

In addition to sensitivity towards emotional characteristic of auditory and visual stimuli, not many studies have discussed the aspect of emotional dependence with field dependence. A study by Konstadt and Forman (1965) was carried out on children who

9

were divided into field-independent and dependent groups with the goal to test the effect of approving and disapproving examiners while the children worked on a routine clerical task. The children who made up the field-independent group were selected based on their higher scores in the Children's Embedded Figures Test(CEFT), while those in the field-dependent group had lower scores in the test. The CEFT is a version of the Embedded Figures Test specifically modified for children after its creation by Witkin to assess field independence and dependence (Karp & Konstadt, 1963). The results showed that performance of field-dependent children reflected more strongly the negative influence of disapproving statements by examiners. The study also recorded the number of gazes by the children at other people as a measure of their affective dependence. The field-dependent children exhibited a greater frequency of gazes than their field-independent counterparts under the condition of disapproval by the examiners. There appeared to be a certain level of emotional engagement as an extension of one's greater sensitivity to social relations. In order to navigate through and achieve one's goals in a maze of potential conflicts within a relationship-oriented social and/or occupational environment, it is necessary to be skillful in attending to and interpreting emotional cues that can be ambiguous at times. In prioritizing relational harmony, the sensitivity towards the emotion of interacting members plays a significant role in its function as an implicit social climate meter, whereby one's detection of positive and/or negative cues would provide useful feedback to decide subsequent action.

The emotional aspect of an interaction can therefore become a salient element within one's scope of perception that moderates the level of assurance of one's optimum social performance. It also shows that emotional and field dependencies may be closely linked in not only a cultural but also a psychosocial dimension. This could be accounted for by a widely distributed neural system for emotion perception in the brain (Phillips, Drevets, Rauch, & Lane, 2003). It can be seen that field-dependent and holistic individuals have the propensity for emotional awareness, which is likely enhanced by cultural norms and social experiences. Such awareness or sensitivity is less pronounced in Western

10

individuals and may provide practical support to the perceptual style that East Asians are accustomed to.

Further, it may be argued that vulnerable young children who participated might have expressed greater emotional needs to a greater degree than adults. However, the purpose of comparison between field-dependent and field-independent children was achieved and the spontaneous display of emotional reliance could offer a better glimpse at the type of possible suppressed response in adults who are more capable of inhibiting expressions in their behaviour. Since Westerners are found to be more field-independent, the results of Konstadt and Forman's study suggest that the children's field-dependent perceptual tendency and relational orientation will also likely wane as they grow older and become accustomed to an individualistic mindset across life domains (Witkin & Berry, 1975). Field dependency is subject to variation in social influence, whether it is by Western independent upbringing or East Asian interdependent culture, despite being observable and assessable by CEFT at a young age.

Emotion as an Interactive and Unifying Component in the Context of Relations

We have seen that individuals' social orientation and vocation play a part in determining their field dependency and holistic perception, which in turn help them to adapt to the needs and demands of the cultural environment in which they live. Our perceptual tendency interacts with culture on a continual basis and beneath the external side of social interactions, it is worthwhile to consider how such active processes are built upon underlying psychological mechanisms, in particular under the East-Asian relationship-oriented environment. The emotional aspect is a potential factor for further exploration to achieve a better understanding of mechanisms that may have a role in consolidating our social orientation and perception.

The greater tendency of emotion perception in field-dependent and holistic study participants implies a seldom studied correlation between emotional saliency and perceptual orientation. Vuilleumier and Driver (2007) discovered that the emotional significance of visual stimuli influenced perceptual processing at the neural level, with enhanced and prolonged responses. Just as social relationships are built upon our sensitivity and responses towards one another's emotions, the interconnectedness between objects in our perceptual field may be supplied by a unifying factor of emotional quality. Thus, emotional salience provides an advantage in the tendency of perceiving interactive relationships between elements. Uchida, Townsend, Markus and Bergsleker (2009) analyzed television interviews of Japanese and American Olympic athletes and studied participants' descriptions of these athletes and their reactions to winning. The results showed that both the athletes and participants of Japanese descent, compared to those of American descent, associated more emotions with relationships; for example, they included people other than the individuals of interest when they described the athletes' emotional reaction to their victory and group pictures with teammates. The authors concluded that the Japanese perceived emotion as relational in nature and jointly shared with others while the Americans saw emotion as originating from within them and being distinctly separated from others. Thus, under such a context, the Japanese may not be less emotional in their expression than their American counterparts. These findings suggest that emotions can carry a more holistic meaning and significance for Asians than previously assumed.

Holistic Perception and Environmental Stimuli in East Asian Cities

The application of holistic perceptual style has also been explicitly expressed in Eastern aesthetic art, which in turn provided further opportunities to perpetuate holistic perception in their audience and followers (Heine, 2012). Similarly, in a study by Nisbett and Miyamoto (2005), comparisons between typical matched cities in the East and West showed that many background structures and objects along sidewalks in Japan are uncommon in American cities. From paired research photographs taken of city scenes, more displays of street advertisements with enlarged wording were observed in the Japanese city, which sought to attract the visual attention of people in the area. The printed advertisement messages arrayed along the streets conveyed a greater amount of informational stimuli than in a typical Western city scene. Thus, holistic perception has led to the development of a form of expression through which the medium of its promotive culture produces psychosocial influence on a readily receptive audience. In East Asian societies where printed advertisements are more prevalent, such objects of holistic expression indirectly help maintain a lively attention-stimulating atmosphere that motivates people to communicate and share their time in relationship-bonding activities. The advertisement displays tend to be found massed together in an area, which can also imply a cultural prioritization of closeness and frequent convening of related group members.

On the other hand, it can be understood that through an extended duration of visual exposure to such an abundant and, at times, overwhelming mass of stimuli that direct relevant and rewarding messages to the viewer (e.g., new products and price discounts), a holistic perceptual style is nurtured for apparent self-benefits. Reinforcement can be in effect, encouraging one to act and obtain benefits from the rewarding positive information offered. In a series of experiments by Seitz, Kim and Watanabe (2009), adult participants were found to be capable of visual perceptual learning in the absence of behavioural task engagement when they were only shown visual stimuli paired with offer of physical rewards. The participants' visual sensitivity was tested by their ability to discriminate correctly the orientations of two sets of stimuli of sinusoidal gratings that were each paired with or without a water reward. The results illustrated that the participants' test performances on the paired stimuli-reward grating orientation were improved from those completed prior to the experiment sessions as compared with those of the unpaired stimuli, which did not show any change. This indicated that learning had taken place in visual perception which bypassed the engagement of behavioural task and intentional decision-making process. Additionally, the technique of continuous flash suppression (CFS), in which presentation of rapidly changing stimuli to one eye suppresses conscious awareness of the presentation of a static stimulus to the other eye, was implemented in one of the experiments to suppress the participants' direct awareness of the stimuli-reward pairing and grating orientation. Still, similar pattern of performance results were obtained. The study shows a fundamental perceptual mechanism at work beyond one's conscious awareness and control. Reward learning could have resulted from the process of visual perception in an environment where there is a crowded presentation of stimuli and an offer of potential rewards to compete for one's attentional focus, irrespective of active task performance. This is to extend the concept of traditional understanding further to the idea that deliberate effort is just one of the routes by which our sensory perceptual process operates; the role of reinforcement in the conditioning of our visual response is just beginning to be explored. With one's long-term exposure to an excessive load of visual stimuli, the content of which can eventually make their way into our cognitive processing stream, it is reasonable to assume that a majority of our perceptual learning actually takes place underneath conscious awareness.

Focus on Background and Foreground of Visual Field

A distinguishing aspect of holistic perceptual style is the subject's attentional focus on both the background and foreground objects of his visual field. A study by Boduroglu, Shah, and Nisbett (2009) hypothesized that East Asians' tendency to focus additionally on the background could be due to their broader scope of visual attention allocation. The results confirmed such by showing that, compared with American participants, East Asians performed better on colour change detection tasks which involved expansion of object positions from their initially closely-spaced distances. When the procedure was

14

reversed (i.e. shrinking the positions of objects that were first displayed as farther apart from one another), East Asian participants performed worse than American participants. With one's frequent exposure and alertness to a greater number of background objects and structures in the environment that carry mentally stimulating messages while having to search for and make judgements on the best choice of displays, this perceptual and cognitive processing tendency can be a likely contributing factor to East Asians' wider attentional breadth.

Additionally, in a comparison between Chinese Singaporean and Caucasian American participants, Goh, Tan, and Park (2009) found greater distance coverage of eye movements as well as a greater proportion of gaze saccades which alternated between objects and backgrounds in pictures when presented to the former group than the latter. This could imply that the tendency to draw associations between objects and backgrounds or the variation across their boundaries may have attracted more of the Chinese Sinagporean participants' attention. From such observation, one can reason that there is a close overlap between field-dependent and object-background crossover perceptual processes.

On the one hand, it is still unclear what specific mechanisms underlie East Asians' preference for greater visual focus and attention on the background than concentrating on foreground stimuli. It is certainly more complex than deliberate effort. Chua, Boland, and Nisbett (2005) found that Chinese participants made more saccadic eye movements than American participants on complex realistic background of pictures with a single foreground object. In the sample pictures presented in this study, the backgrounds contained a greater variety of multi-coloured visual details. It is worth considering whether the preference for variety in objects' attributes and a broader range of distinct visual qualities carry more positive meanings, such as harmony and completeness of one's group, to East Asians who reflexively prolonged their attention. A study which examined European Americans and East Asians' coloring works on geometric patterns showed that East Asians selected more colours and produced colorings which were judged to be more harmonious than the unique and higher hue-contrast works of the American participants (Ishii, Miyamoto, Rule, & Toriyama, 2014).

As an example, a random selection of a pair of artwork by two popular American and Japanese artists obtained freely from the web showed distinctive colour use strategies by their creators. In the case of the famous American painter, his artwork presented an excessive use of only three colours (as analysed by an online colour palette extractor, Version 1.0 TinEye Multicolor Engine, 2020), which are brown, black and grey, with the most used colour brown accounting for about 80% of his full image. In contrast, the paired contemporary Japanese painter only used 10.8% of the colour brown in his randomly selected artwork, along with an evenly distributed usage of eight other colours, most of them having bright hues (See Figures 1 and 2). This random comparison offers us a subtle glimmer of the distinctive application and selective preference of colours between Eastern and Western cultures, which paints a clear emphasis on difference(s) in terms of the concept of diversity or variation in art less frequently discussed in the academic realm. Intuitively, the East-Asian culture which upholds harmony and connection among its people may attempt to compensate for a high degree of similarity in community attitude and values with greater distinctiveness and variation in its artistic expression, which has just the opposite effect in its Western counterpart. In a subconscious effort to compensate for the greater level of individualism and achievement for personal distinctiveness by Westerners, this effect may spill over to express more similarity in artistic product in order to strike a balance between our quest for distinction and connection. In simple terms, we want to perceive and produce a healthy balance between differences and sameness in our world and creations. Hence, culture speaks to what we value and strive to achieve, not only as a group, but as individuals who both share and stand out to voice for the common good.

Color map regions   Proportional palette

For Sample 1 artwork by a randomly selected American artist A1.

28.8 %	#676337	Brown
20.1 %	#403a26	Brown
19.0 %	#2a2a22	Black
10.6 %	#857b35	Brown
9.3 %	#4d4221	Brown
4.0 %	#b69f44	Brown
3.6 %	#8c4631	Brown
1.7 %	#805634	Brown
1.5 %	#e9dcaf	Grey
1.4 %	#b9ad74	Brown

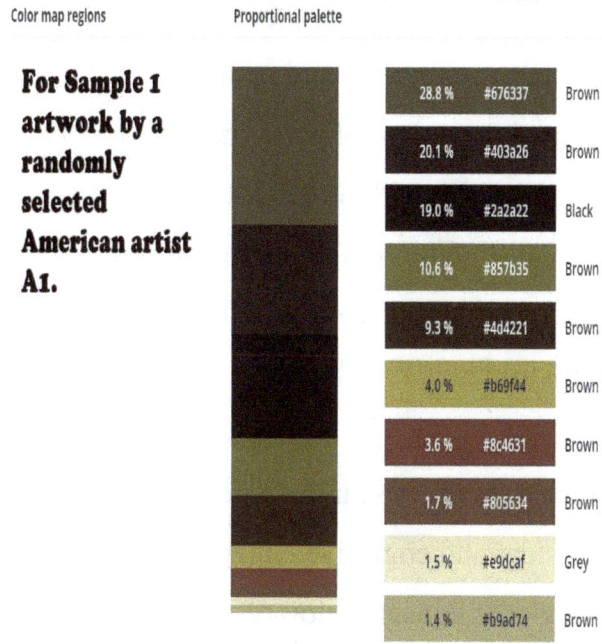

Figure 1 Colour extraction analysis of artwork by an American artist.

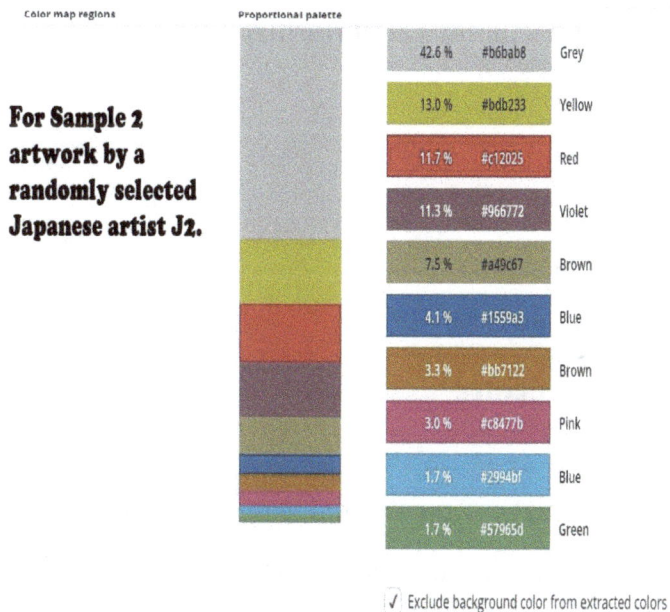

Color map regions   Proportional palette

For Sample 2 artwork by a randomly selected Japanese artist J2.

42.6 %	#b6bab8	Grey
13.0 %	#bdb233	Yellow
11.7 %	#c12025	Red
11.3 %	#966772	Violet
7.5 %	#a49c67	Brown
4.1 %	#1559a3	Blue
3.3 %	#bb7122	Brown
3.0 %	#c8477b	Pink
1.7 %	#2994bf	Blue
1.7 %	#57965d	Green

✓ Exclude background color from extracted colors

Figure 2 Colour extraction analysis of artwork by a Japanese artist.

From the previous study by Nisbett and Miyamoto (2005), the background of Japanese city scenes presented a variety of sign displays in a number of attractive shades of

17

colours. The influence of traditional cultural values and beliefs pertaining to relationship orientation may therefore play a role in the colour preferences and applications. On the other hand, research has not clearly differentiated the extent of participants' focus on visual stimuli with attributes that bear more similarities with those that are more distinctly varied. Should future studies be able to shed more light on this aspect, we may be closer to deciphering another underlying perceptual mechanism that characterizes the holistic style and connects with the Eastern environmental influence.

With respect to external environmental influence, future research could address the possibility of one's greater activation of perceptual and cognitive engagement while being in a typical East Asian environment. In addition, the consideration of ambient auditory stimuli and their effect when combined with visual objects could offer a more complete understanding of overall environmental impact. Not only are East Asian city scenes more visually stimulating, but such environments can also be teeming with richer amounts of auditory stimuli when relationship-bonding opportunities are prioritized.

Possible Sensitive Period in Perceptual Style

Development, Parental Roles and Family Structure

There are sensitive periods for culture and language acquisition during one's early years of development prior to full adulthood, and the extent to which these sensitive periods would affect the establishment of a person's perceptual style and cognition when the young brain is particularly most receptive remains to be explored (Heine, 2012). The earlier section of this paper has pointed out that field dependence can be nurtured and enhanced by cultural and psychological factors. It is not unique to the Eastern culture, however, as certain sub-Western cultures exhibit collectivism to a greater degree than others.

Recent research on the impact of culture on one's sensitive developmental period has focused on maternal upbringing with children (Wang, 2006). In contrast, paternal influence has been less studied within the context of culture, and so are the differences between Western and Eastern children's views and expectations of their fathers towards themselves and the family. Paternal participation in a child's growth and development can vary in their activeness, which could be challenging in the face of modern culture, where men and women live in societies that endorse different levels and aspects of gender equality. Canadian statistics showed that the number of single-parent families had risen by 8.0% between the years 2006 and 2011, with those headed by single mothers making up 80.0% of them in 2011 (Statistics Canada, 2015). In East Asia, the rates of divorce, and the resulting single parenthood, have risen in major industrialized countries such as China, where the divorce rates used to be almost zero in the 1970s (Yeung & Park, 2015). For the average Eastern family, the impacts of placing the father as the central authority figure should also be considered and studied according to the context of a rapidly modernized and globally-connected Asian society. Complex emotional and social issues can affect the stages of children's development when parental roles can be switched, substituted, or not assumed by physically and/or emotionally absent fathers and mothers.

A longitudinal study by Schacht, Cummings, and Davies (2009) reported that children's emotional security played a mediating role in the relationship between their fathers' behavior and their own development. Fathers help determine their children's style of attachment security and dependence (Howard, 2009). From a practical point of view, parental upbringing may not appear as solid and stable as it is generally presumed to be. Globalization sees the developing Eastern world encountering and assimilating Western influence of tradition-contradicting lifestyle and opinions. Parental affirmation and criticism regulate the emotional climate in the home, influencing the children's sense of security during a period when they are most sensitive to culture acquisition. As Eastern families become more subjected to Western influence which alters paternal roles, future research should consider whether a vulnerable level of emotional security due to inadequate or irregular parental participation during a child's period of development may be linked to greater emotional dependency, which as we have seen, is related to field dependence tendency.

Conclusion and Future Directions

Both social and environmental factors work hand in hand to reinforce holistic perception in people of cultural groups characterized by interdependence and harmonious relations. A tendency of holistic perceptual style, field dependence, may lead to the utilization of a greater degree of emotional dependency and sensitivity towards affective expressions and cues from others in order to maintain social order and avoid conflict. Although research has focused on the emotional suppression tendency of East Asians, their moderation in explicit expression through channel(s) unfamiliar to Western societies may mask their underlying sensitivity towards perception of emotion in others.

The immediate and frequent exposure to East Asian cities provide a considerable variety of informational stimuli to play a significant role in their residents' expanded attentional breadth and greater frequency of object-crossing-background visual processing. One challenge is to determine at which point in time such visual processing becomes a deliberate effort following spontaneous attentional allocation. It would be useful if the broad definition of holistic perceptual style could be clearer in identifying its distinct components and distinguishing between object-object and object-background visual focus. It would also be useful to investigate whether individuals with a holistic perceptual style attend more to the variation or similarity between visual stimuli, be that the background or foreground object in a field. Such division or categorization could expand the discussion and shed light on the common denominator as well as presently unclear distinction between field dependence (also exhibited by Westerners) and Easterners' holistic perception. Further studies could determine the association between non-emotional neutral stimuli and visual perception of a relational context, particularly in holistic perceivers. Furthermore, the concept of field dependence and holistic perception could be extended to focus on stimuli of audible nature. Similar to the contrast in city scenes between a Western and an East Asian environment, ambient noise is more intense and cognitively stimulating in the latter than the former. Culturally nurtured perceptual style can then be likened to a versatile mold that accommodates a range of stimuli streaming through more than one sensory faculty. Lastly, since Easterners are particularly receptive to the perpetuation of holistic perception through generations, future research could look more into the the mutually enhancing properties and intertwining of external environmental elements (as an expression and channel of survival of culture) with psychosocial factors, as opposed to addressing these aspects separately.

Western Analytical Versus Eastern Holistic Perception and Cognition

Based on the results of a simplified Rod and Frame test carried out on Western and non-Western volunteers, the former group was discovered to performed overall better than the former. What follows is a discussion of the cultural factor that could account for the difference in scores between participants of Western and non-Western descent.

People from Western cultural background are more able to focus with greater ease than non-Westerners and separate out the target rod from other miscellaneous images in the background. This is due to their analytical thinking tendency which leads them to perceive each object individually and discretely by categorizing them according to their properties and relevant abstract rules (Heine, 2012). In this case of Rod and Frame test, the orange target rod was effortlessly seen by Western participants as uniquely distinct from the rest of the picture which dominated their attention and more than 40% of them remarked that it was not at all difficult to answer the questions posed. On the other hand, non-Western participants with their holistic perception style, attended more to the entire visual information of the pictures which added to their difficulty and inaccuracy in detecting the subtle rod's angle of deviation from the horizontal and vertical. They might have looked more at the distracting background, which purposefully misled them, than the target rod just like the Chinese subjects did in a study by Chua, Boland, & Nisbett (as cited in Heine, 2012).

Based on a set of full correct responses by an Asian participant who reasoned that his years of technical occupational background, which required strong analytical expertise, enabled him to answer accurately all questions of the test, it appears that culturally-influenced perceptual styles affect people to varying degree regardless of the group you were born into. There are other aspects of life which can significantly sharpen our unique cognitive skills and influence our performance in judging specific attributes of target stimuli, depending on the amount of time we devote to such processes in bringing about the change, as evident in the results of priming in the above studies.

The holistic tendency to attend to background details and, if not more than, the foreground objects has its influences, just as much as analytical thinking also does, which pervade various aspects of life in the non-Western and Western worlds respectively. Intuitively, a holistic perceptual tendency also emphasises integration, interconnection, unity and harmony of elements, a globalised focus and a prioritisation of inclusion over exclusion of members that values belonging and participation. It could be for this purpose that familial importance and precedence are held in high regard in the Eastern community for the primary benefits of members, both young and old. We could observe this in a very concrete way from the fact that family surnames are addressed first and foremost before the given names of individuals in East-Asian countries while the opposite practice of addressing given names before family names is the Western norm. However, it is also interesting to note that there are ethnic groups in other parts of Asia where a history of Westernised influence pervades and follow the practice of writing given names before family names. The prevalence of family names before given names is therefore a firmly established tradition and strict cultural and ethnic representation of the East-Asian societies, i.e. Chinese, Korean and Japanese, which highly esteem Confucian values and moral principles.

Another perceptual and cognitive aspect - relational thinking style of non-Westerners with probable cultural basis of influence, could be attributed to childhood upbringing by mothers. Tardif and her colleagues reported that non-Western mothers (as cited in Nisbett, & Miyamoto, 2005) speak of more verbs which emphasise relations amongst objects and/or people. Another study by Wang & Ross also observed (as cited in Wang, 2006) that Chinese mothers talked with their children about past events with greater social-relational context. On the other hand, North American children displayed noun bias which could be the result of their mothers' frequent use of nouns during conversations with them along with the habit of labeling toys and calling their attention to the objects' attributes (Heine, 2012; Nisbett, & Miyamoto, 2005). Such noun bias could proceed to promote a form of language bias in Westerners in which the preference for language expression and explicitness by way of noun labeling and rich verbal description and narration hold an important and significant cultural seat in the lives of Western Europeans. The contrasting maternal influence between Westerners and non-Westerners thus extends even into adulthood and can chronically affect cognition and perception. Apart from the spoken language, there are also variations in the forms of written language which people in different parts of the world are exposed to on a daily basis. A functional MRI study of native Chinese speakers from China which examined brain asymmetry during the processing of Chinese characters found significant activation of the right occipital region in contrast with the left for alphabetic languages like English (Xue et al., 2005). This supports that the visuospatial properties of Chinese characters demand for more right-hemispheric dominant holistic processing. In addition, holistic thinking style also has been explicitly expressed in Eastern aesthetic art which in turn provided even more opportunities to positively encourage holistic perception in viewers somewhat like a continual cycle (Heine, 2012). In a group of three studies by Krishna, Zhou, & Zhang (2008), they tested the effect of holistic and analytic perceptual styles on the spatial judgement biases of mainland Chinese and American students. As expected, the results showed that direct distance bias, which they hypothesized to be likely to occur when a person fails to attend to context-relevant information in their judgement, was demonstrated more by the Americans than Chinese. In their second study, when the subjects were primed by reading articles and word search tasks which focused on independent and interdependent themes respectively, those in the former group condition displayed greater direct distance bias.

Another example of experience which could produce different responses to the test is the city scenes which people are exposed to daily. According to Miyamoto and Nisbett (as cited in Heine, 2012), Western cities, compared with Eastern ones of Japan, are less complex and busy with noticeably less number of background structures and objects. A study which tested the impact of such city scenes on the attentional styles of Japanese and Americans discovered that pictures of busier Japanese cities could possibly affect the Americans, apart from the Japanese, to be more holistic in their perception. In addition, the concept and values of communalism, connection and unity of Eastern culture(s) can be reflected in the architectural makeup and designs of traditional abode – each living unit and room component in a setting is well-connected (as opposed to well-"distributed" in the West) and closely integrated through easily accessible and reachable hallways, open corridors and passages. Even moreso, they lead to the central courtyard, a convening "staple" destination for the close-knitted abode community. The floors of each group home setting are also lowly elevated from the ground without regard for great heights, an intuitive reminder of the Eastern cherished value of "lowliness" and self-humility. A practical example of this East-West distinction is the extensive use of high and narrow-width towers in traditional and orthodox Western architecture as opposed to broad and wide widths with low preference for great heights of buildings in the East. One can come across them frequently in the castles and churches of Europe and compare them with the appearance of imperial Chinese and Japanese palaces in Asia. This denotes the lesser importance of the centre of gravity stability in Western architectural construction as this characteristic is more vulnerable in high and that the mission of "soaring to great heights" is prized more, hence reflected in the physical display of such buildings. Perhaps, stability through the course of time and being deeply rooted and grounded in traditions and culture are valuable and highly esteemed in the East, thus great buildings there are well modeled after this principle, e.g. broad base at the expense of towering heights. In addition, humility and lowliness as prized and practical virtues speak to this regard. Extended kinship and point of connectedness between fellow men, when visualized diagrammatically, tend to spread and multiply in number and radially moreso on a horizontal basis, which reminds of the Eastern preference for a broad base foundational structure. The opposite seems to be in application in the West, where the horizontal basis of connections between immediate and adjacent points of contacts(persons) is decreased in number within a tall and narrow spatial structure where one's gaze or visual field is intensively focused either upwards(as if denoting expectation and prestige of achievement) or downwards(those at a lower grade from self) in a longitudinal direction. In such a longitudinal spatial confinement, a person has a greater awareness or consciousness of the self(himself/herself) because when stationed on a single floor level of a tower chamber, there is less breadth of a space for others on the same level to be present and seen by oneself. It is therefore no surprise to observe that circular round shaped tables are frequently used for family and community dining in the East more than long rectangular tables. When gathered together at large round tables, their shape without pointed ends or corners represents proximity, connectedness, continuity and lasting relationships like a circle without end. Furthermore, one's visual field when seated by a circular table reaches every other single person all around, therefore everyone is valued and very well visually represented in close unity and cherished interactions. This advantage is greatly sacrificed for members seated down a long rectangular table where one's horizontal(left-right) visual field of all members is obstructed. Another Easterners' advantage is that the food served on a round table is within everyone's reach of equal distance(all at similar lengths of radius) as members are seated at the same distance from the centre of the table. This is especially practical as everyone eats from and shares the same dishes of main course, which is in an opposite individual style of Western dining where the act and style of sharing are minimally encouraged. Individualism and the process of separation and division are an inclination that is very much built-in in Western culture and living. Take for instance, the most important celebration event in a person's life, one's birthday, and the act of cutting a cake is symbolic of separation and division of a wholesome birthday cake into individual or isolated slices. A counter example from the East brings to mind the popular street food of a few fishballs or meatballs which are "connected" or joined together in one single skewer stick when served and eaten.

Figure 3:The West: To Cut

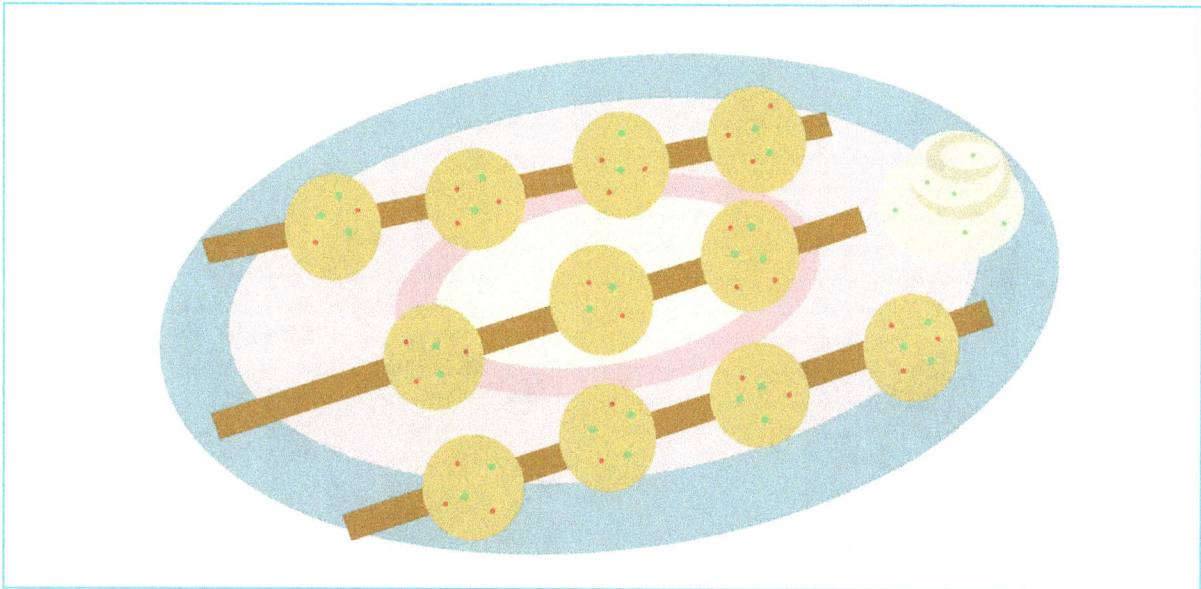

Figure 4: The East: To Connect

Not surprisingly, cutting food with knives and forks, and the act of holding together with a pair of "connected" chopsticks and spoon paint a striking picture of contrast at the Western and Eastern meal table. Even under various education disciplines and professional lines of work, the West has been dividing and branching out into numerous subgroups on a more extensive basis in recent times than interconnecting them all.

In terms of other trivial East-West distinctions, one can also look at the basis of material used to fashion their cutlery. Easterners gather such from soft, light and flexible strength and cost-saving material such as wood(e.g. chopsticks), clay(e.g. claypot), bamboo(e.g. steamers) and leaves. On the other hand, the West prefers tough and expensive metal, silver and iron. This may bring us to the preliminary analysis of the cultural differences in terms of approach and attitude towards cost expenditure and material preference for the degree of flexibility and strength. The greater the flexibility, the lesser the strength, and vice versa. Our forefathers had decided on such and in doing so, paved the way for the future, i.e. our present-day distinctive cultural assets.

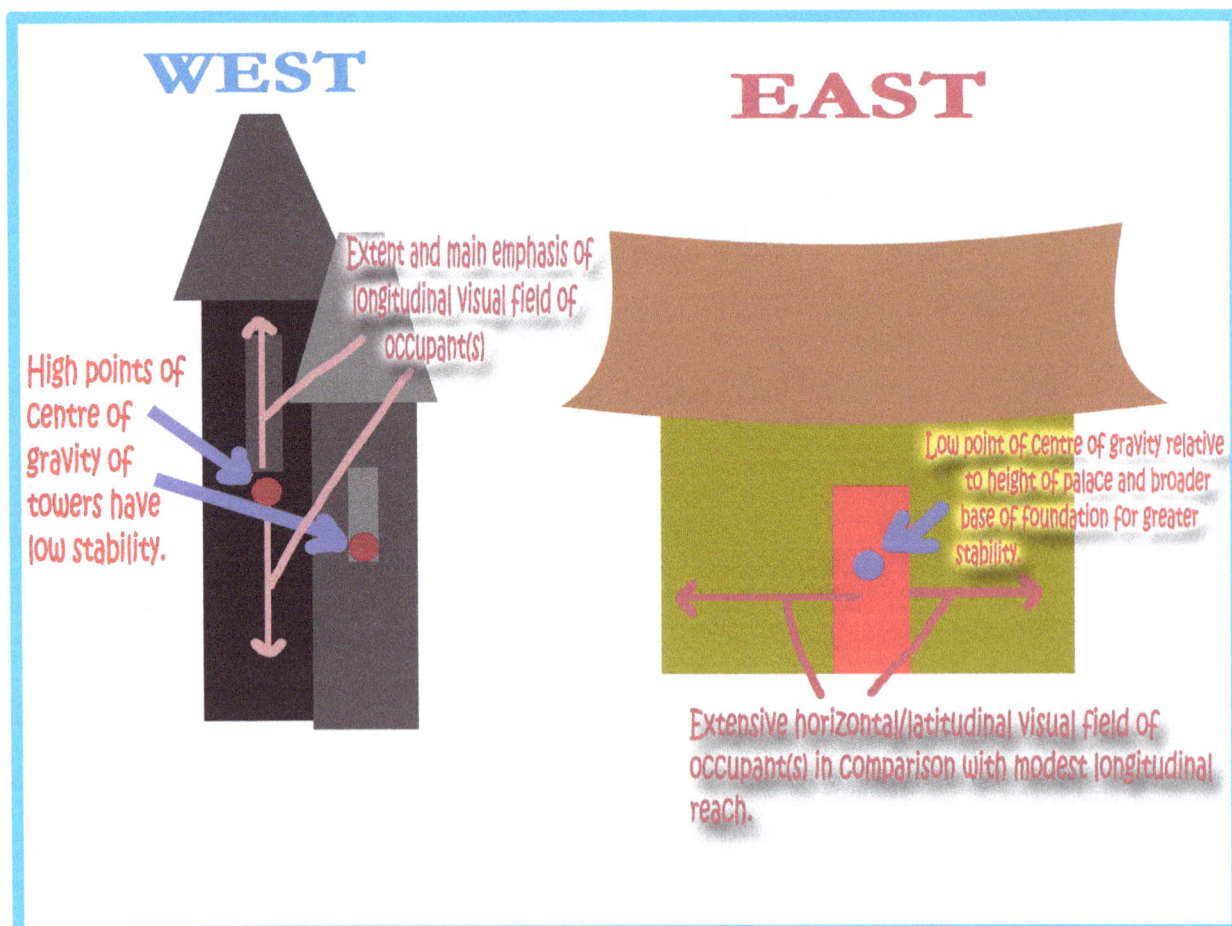

WEST

EAST

Extent and main emphasis of longitudinal visual field of occupant(s)

High points of centre of gravity of towers have low stability.

Low point of centre of gravity relative to height of palace and broader base of foundation for greater stability.

Extensive horizontal/latitudinal visual field of occupant(s) in comparison with modest longitudinal reach.

Figure 5 Distinctive East-West architectural traditions.

28

References

Chua, H. F., Boland, J. E., & Nisbett, R. E. (2005). Cultural variation in eye movements during scene perception. *Proceedings of the National Academy of Sciences of the United States of America, 102,* 12629-12633. doi:10.1073/pnas.0506162102

Chua, H. F., Leu, J., & Nisbett, R. E. (2005). Culture and diverging views of social events. *Personality and Social Psychology Bulletin, 31,* 925-934. doi:10.1177/0146167204272166

Boduroglu, A., Shah, P., & Nisbett, R. E. (2009). Cultural differences in allocation of attention in visual information processing. *Journal of Cross-Cultural Psychology, 40,* 349-360. doi:10.1177/0022022108331005

Goh, J. O., Tan, J. C., & Park, D. C. (2009). Culture modulates eye-movements to visual novelty. *PLoS ONE, 4,* e8238. doi:10.1371/journal.pone.0008238

Heine, S. J. (2010). Cultural psychology. In S. T. Fiske, D. T. Gilbert, & G. Linzey (Eds.), *Handbook of social psychology* (pp. 1423-1464). Hoboken, NJ: John Wiley & Sons.

Heine, S. J. (2012). *Cultural psychology.* New York, N.Y.: W.W. Norton.

Ishii, K., Miyamoto, Y., Rule, N. O., & Toriyama, R. (2014). Physical objects as vehicles of cultural transmission: Maintaining harmony and uniqueness through colored geometric patterns. *Personality and Social Psychology Bulletin, 40*(2), 175-188. doi: 10.1177/0146167213508151

Karp, S. A., & Konstadt, N. L. (1963). Manual for the Children's Embedded Figures Test.

Kitayama, S., & Ishii, K. (2002). Word And voice: Spontaneous attention to emotional utterances in two languages. *Cognition and Emotion, 16*(1), 29-

59. doi:10.1080/0269993943000121

Konstadt, N., & Forman, E. (1965). Field dependence and external directedness. *Journal of Personality and Social Psychology, 1,* 490-493. doi:10.1037/h0021875

Krishna, A., Zhou, R., & Zhang, S. (2008). The effect of self-construal on spatial judgments. *Journal of Consumer Research, 35,* 337-348. doi:10.1086/588686

Masuda, T., & Nisbett, R. E. (2001). Attending holistically versus analytically: Comparing the context sensitivity of Japanese and Americans. *Journal of Personality and Social Psychology, 81,* 922-934. doi:10.1037/0022-3514.81.5.922

Nisbett, R. E., & Miyamoto, Y. (2005). The influence of culture: Holistic versus analytic perception. *Trends in Cognitive Sciences, 9,* 467-473. doi:10.1016/j.tics.2005.08.004

Norenzayan, A., Choi, I., & Peng, K. (2007). Perception and cognition. In S. Kitayama & D. Cohen (Eds.), *Handbook of cultural psychology* (pp. 569-594). New York, NY: The Guilford Press.

Phillips, M. L., Drevets, W. C., Rauch, S. L., & Lane, R. (2003). Neurobiology of emotion perception I: The neural basis of normal emotion perception. *Biological psychiatry, 54*(5), 504-514. doi:10.1016/S0006-3223(03)00168-9

Schacht, P. M., Cummings, E. M., & Davies, P. T. (2009). Fathering in family context and child adjustment: A longitudinal analysis. *Journal of Family Psychology, 23*(6), 790.

Seitz, A. R., Kim, D., & Watanabe, T. (2009). Rewards evoke learning of unconsciously processed visual stimuli in adult humans. *Neuron, 61,* 700-707. doi:10.1016/j.neuron.2009.01.016

Sekiyama, K., & Tohkura, Y. (1991). McGurk effect in non-English listeners: Few visual effects for Japanese subjects hearing Japanese syllables of high auditory intelligibility. *Journal of the Acoustical Society of America, 90,* 1797-1805. doi:10.1121/1.401660

Statistics Canada. (2015). *Portrait of families and living arrangements in Canada.* Retrieved from http://www12.statcan.gc.ca/census-recensement/2011/as-sa/98-312-x/98-312-x2011001-eng.cfm

Tanaka, A., Koizumi, A., Imai, H., Hiramatsu, S., Hiramoto, E., & de Gelder, B. (2010). I feel your voice: Cultural differences in the multisensory perception of emotion. *Psychological Science, 21,* 1259-1262. doi:10.1177/0956797610380698

TinEye Lab Multicolor Engine [Computer software]. (2020). Retrieved from https://labs.tineye.com/color

Uchida, Y., Townsend, S. S. M., Markus, H. R., & Bergsieker, H. B. (2009). Emotions as within or between people? Cultural variation in lay theories of emotion expression and inference. *Personality & Social Psychology Bulletin, 35,* 1427-1439. doi:10.1177/0146167209347322

Vuilleumier, P., & Driver, J. (2007). Modulation of visual processing by attention and emotion: Windows on causal interactions between human brain regions. *Philosophical Transactions: Biological Sciences, 362,* 837-855. Retrieved from http://www.jstor.org/stable/20209893

Wang, Q. (2006). Culture and the development of self-knowledge. *Current Directions in Psychological Science, 15,* 182-187. doi:10.1111/j.1467-8721.2006.00432.x

Witkin, H. A., & Berry, J. W. (1975). Psychological differentiation in cross-cultural perspective. *Journal of Cross Cultural Psychology, 6,* 4-87

Witkin, H. A., Dyk, R. B., Faterson, H. F., Goodenough, D. R., & Karp, S. A. (1974). *Psychological differentiation.* Potomac, Md: Lawrence Erlbaum Assoc.

Xue, G., Dong, Q., Chen, K., Jin, Z., Chen, C., Zeng, Y., & Reiman, E. M. (2005). Cerebral asymmetry in children when reading Chinese characters. *Cognitive Brain Research, 24,* 206-214. doi:10.1016/j.cogbrainres.2005.01.022

Yeung, W. J., & Park, H. (2016). Growing Up in One-Parent Families in Asia. *Marriage & Family Review, 52*(1-2), 1-14.